The Handbook of Emotionally Intelligent Leadership

Inspiring Others to Achieve Results

Daniel A. Feldman, Ph.D.

To order additional copies of *The Handbook of Emotionally Intelligent Leadership,* fax the order form in the back of this book or call **1.800.511.6150**. For more information about our programs on increasing emotional intelligence in the workplace, call us or visit our website at

www.leadershipperformance.com

Contents

"The leader's fundamental act is to induce people to be aware or conscious of what they feel — to feel their true needs so strongly, to define their values so meaningfully, that they can be moved to purposeful action."[1]

James MacGregor Burns

Chapter I

Leadership
and
Emotional
Intelligence

We know effective leadership when we experience it. We feel the pull of leadership when we're working with someone we trust and we want to do things that please that person. We feel it when we meet someone who has a vision about what they want to achieve in the short and long term and who, at the same time, is also able to see other peoples' points of view.

A senior executive, seeking a new position, interviewed with the vice president of a healthcare organization. The applicant said that she really wanted to work for this VP because of the sense of leadership that emanated from her. The executive said of the VP, "She's someone you really want to please. You feel captured by her intelligence. She is very clear about where she is going. She has a quiet enthusiasm."

Leadership is about a person having the power to influence others. Two types of power are particularly important. There is the power that derives from an assigned, formal position. And then there is the power that arises out of the relationship between two people. This personal power that comes from a relationship is a key factor in effective leadership. A leader's personal power is the power freely given to the leader by others. Effective leaders focus on their personal power - their relationship power - more than their position power.

John, a senior manager at a large computer service organization, walked into an explosion. Two of his subordinates were at each other's throats. Bob, the newest member of John's work group, was near apoplexy.

2

Bob said,
> *"I've had it with Barbara Bennett's snippy, self-serving comments!"*

Barbara said,
> *"I'm fed up with Bob -- He just has no long-term focus!"*

Instead of avoiding the situation or blowing up, John sat down with the two of them.   He calmly said, "Together, we are going to reach an understanding of the core problems you two are having. And we're going to keep working at it until we figure out a way for the two of you to be able to work together closely and successfully." After the one-hour meeting Barbara and John walked out the door, enthusiastically discussing how great it was that they each brought so much to the table.

Effective leadership doesn't happen just because someone has a long-range vision. It happens in the moment-to-moment incidents of our work lives. Effective leadership evolves from all our decisions, big and small. It unfolds through all our interactions with the people with whom we work. Leadership is demonstrated as much in the way we greet people as we pass them casually in the hall as by our demeanor when we describe the new direction for an organization to a five-hundred person division.

So what is effective leadership and how can we learn to exert it? This handbook offers a new approach to answering these questions. It explores effective leadership within the context of emotional intelligence. Leadership aligns people around a shared objective. It is about influencing others to work cooperatively, constructively, and with mutual trust to confront and resolve difficulties and differences.

3

A team of government scientists was formed to provide technical support to administrators concerned with a public health initiative. A new Ph.D. was hired and assigned to the team. He had more education and experience than the others, and this evoked jealousies and competition. A power struggle developed. The supervisor coached the team on working together, but the problems continued. She might then have blown up at the team members and demanded that they all get along. Or, she could have ignored the problem and hoped the team would muddle through.

Instead, she worked to understand the underlying problem and focused on getting to know and establishing rapport with each member of the team. Then she dealt directly and openly with the team about the interpersonal issues. She negotiated agreements on how the team would operate. At the same time, she stayed focused on the tasks and goals the team must ultimately achieve.

Emotionally intelligent leadership is about fully developing and applying our emotional and social skills to effectively influence constructive endeavors in others. It's the personal and "people skills" that are crucial ingredients to effective leadership.

Organizational structures are changing rapidly in all sectors: private, non-profit, and government. The need for emotionally intelligent leadership in organizations is greater today than ever. The nature of work is shifting dramatically. Change now happens much more rapidly than it used to because of the impact of technology, globalization, and new organizational structures such as flattening and de-centralizing.

Large and small, the changes are rolling through the world of work. Author and organizational consultant Peter Vail, a Professor of Human Systems at George Washington University, calls this a "state of permanent white water,"[2] an environment of continual newness.

There are two sets of emotionally intelligent leadership skills. The first set includes the *core skills* of emotional intelligence, crucial to each individual in any workplace endeavor.[3] These are:

- ⮥ Knowing Yourself
- ⮥ Maintaining Control
- ⮥ Reading Others
- ⮥ Perceiving Accurately
- ⮥ Communicating with Flexibility

When we lead others, a second level of skills is necessary along with the core skills. When we employ these skills, we inspire others. These *higher-order skills* are:

- ⮥ Taking Responsibility
- ⮥ Generating Choices
- ⮥ Embracing a Vision
- ⮥ Having Courage
- ⮥ Demonstrating Resolve

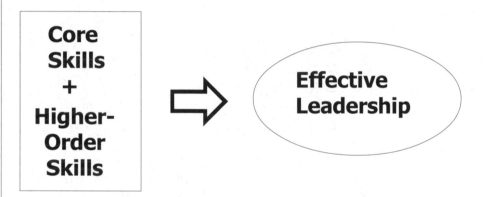

People who demonstrate emotionally intelligent leadership are sensitive to the needs of others and vary their responses according to the situation at hand. They are highly adaptable.

Margaret is a senior executive who joined the public affairs division of a major government agency a couple of years ago. The person she replaced had very little interest or time for the "people" side of the organization. He gave feedback only during the required annual performance review, and that feedback was generally negative.

When Margaret started, she noticed people were very defensive whenever she spoke to them. Taking her time, she gradually introduced more and more informal feedback, positive as well as negative, into discussions. She listened attentively to their reactions and was very responsive to their suggestions.

Meanwhile, Margaret noticed that many of the staff were often late for meetings, so she created systems of accountability for being on time. If someone was late for a meeting, they had to add a quarter to a slush fund for every 5 minutes late. In spite of these new requirement, the workers could tell that Margaret was different, that she cared. In the time Margaret has been at her job, there has been increased productivity and a great demand to be transferred into Margaret's division.

Margaret demonstrated the skills of emotionally intelligent leadership and it paid off with the respect and dedication of her workers. Being an emotionally intelligent leader doesn't mean being a pushover. It takes a willingness to face conflict and persevere to reach a goal.

The computer visionary Esther Dyson has said,

> *"As routine is sucked out of our daily work lives, people who can create stability from chaos will be key."*[4]

Emotionally intelligent leaders can create stability from chaos. In the face of the confusion in many of today's organizations, emotionally intelligent leaders provide the direction and stability that inspires the commitment and motivation crucial to organizational success.

Chapter 2

What is the Role of Emotions in the Workplace?

Emotionally intelligent leadership focuses on using our emotional and relationship "know how" to motivate others to accomplish workplace goals that address the needs of the staff, the organization, and the customer.

To understand emotionally intelligent leadership more fully, let's look at the role of emotions at work. When it comes to the workplace, many people don't want anything to do with emotions. One manager said heatedly, "People should not bring their emotions to work!" The fact is that it's impossible to leave our emotions at home. Even this manager's statement was filled with emotion. Emotions give impact to our decisions, our questions, our instructions. They inform all our actions, our dreams, and our concerns. Emotions are part and parcel of who and what we are.

Emotions affect us whether we are aware of them or not. The ability to feel is hardwired into our physical system. This does not mean that a particular emotion is pre-programmed to happen, but that the ability to experience an emotion is built into us. Emotions are a critical part of what we are as human beings.

People are Theory Makers

➲ As we go through life and work, we take in data that we use to build theories to explain the situations we find ourselves in.

➲ The more data we add, the more accurate is our picture of the world and the better our decision-making process becomes.

➲ Our theories are colored by our feelings and emotional reactions to the things we experience.

Let's experiment with this...

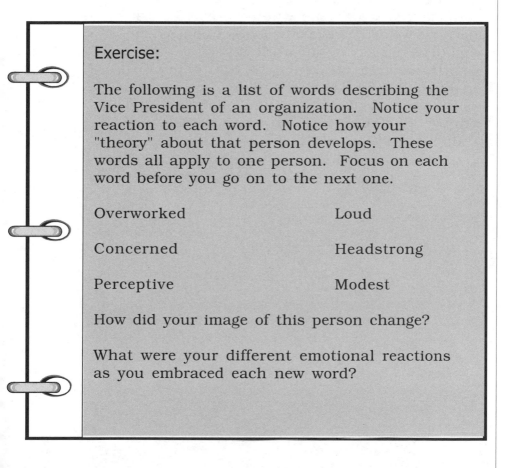

Exercise:

The following is a list of words describing the Vice President of an organization. Notice your reaction to each word. Notice how your "theory" about that person develops. These words all apply to one person. Focus on each word before you go on to the next one.

Overworked	Loud
Concerned	Headstrong
Perceptive	Modest

How did your image of this person change?

What were your different emotional reactions as you embraced each new word?

What are Emotions?

⊃ Emotions are the end result of information processing that has been occurring unconsciously and reflect what has been felt in the body. The response of the body is an integral part of the overall emotional process.

How do we become aware of our emotions? Through what our body tells us. We can't leave our emotions at home when we go to work, because we can't leave our *body* at home. And emotions are key to our work experience. Our emotions give guidance to our decision-making. In the day-to-day decisions such as task selection, delegation, time allotment, and where to focus our attention, we are influenced by our feelings.

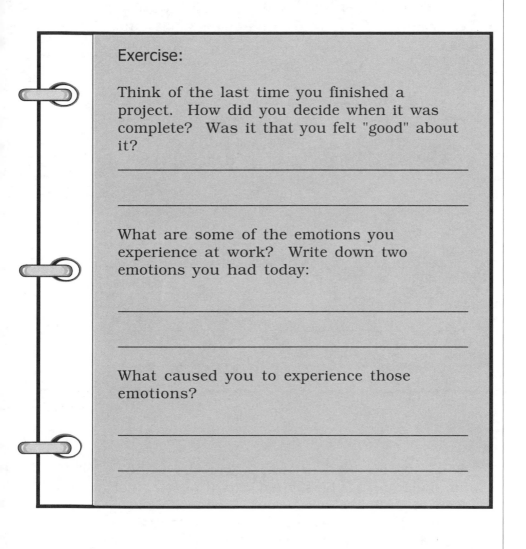

Exercise:

Think of the last time you finished a project. How did you decide when it was complete? Was it that you felt "good" about it?

_____

_____

What are some of the emotions you experience at work? Write down two emotions you had today:

_____

_____

What caused you to experience those emotions?

_____

_____

Exercise:

Let's examine the way that emotions influence performance. Answer the following questions:

What is the effect of anger on performance?

_____

_____

What is the effect of fear on performance?

_____

_____

What is the effect of happiness on performance?

_____

_____

Some people answer that anger disrupts communication. Others point out that it can help to identify problem areas. Some might say fear inhibits you from taking effective action at work. Others say fear moderates inappropriate actions. Some say happiness helps performance by giving a boost of energy, while others point out it can make you giddy and distracted.

This range of possible responses teaches us that emotions aren't inherently good or bad. If we don't pay attention to an emotion, that can hinder our performance; if we get too caught up in an emotion, that can also hinder our performance.

When we are emotionally intelligent, we let ourselves be informed, but not ruled, by our emotions. You probably know some people who have been labeled "too emotional." What is really happening? They are not dealing fully with their feelings, so those feelings burst out and cause problems. Emotional intelligence is about incorporating the message of the emotions in a balanced way so that they support our reasoning.

Although cognitive reasoning (IQ) and emotional intelligence (EI) are distinct from each other, they work together. One reinforces the other. Emotions need to be involved in our decision-making in order for us to successfully navigate life and work. They need to be in balance for us to be most effective. To be in balance with our emotions we need to learn *more* about our emotions rather than ignoring them.

Emotional intelligence is composed of the emotional and social skills through which we cope successfully with the demands of life.

➲ It is being intelligent about our emotional life and relationships.

➲ It is using our emotional and social resources to their fullest.

➲ It gives us a "way point" - a navigational guide - that helps us determine where we are, how far we've come and where to go next.

➲ It is different from personality factors (long-standing traits), and IQ (cognitive intelligence), both of which are fairly stable over a lifetime.

Emotional intelligence skills can be developed throughout life. In fact, research indicates that emotional intelligence can develop well into our adulthood.[5] When we apply our emotional and social skills to *leading* others in the workplace, we are demonstrating emotionally intelligent leadership.

Chapter 3

Blocks to Emotional Intelligence

At work a variety of factors may keep us from taking effective action. Work is important to our sense of security, our need for achievement, and our need for acceptance by others. Consequently, when these needs are threatened a number of habitual protective patterns often come into play.

Exercise:

Let's look at some specific examples of blocks to being effective at work.

Ask yourself this question -- "What stops me from taking effective action?"

Situation	What stops me?
Example: Late on budget project	Avoiding difficult choices

Following are some of the underlying habitual patterns that block the use of our emotional intelligence.

Fear and Worry

Fear can be enormously limiting. When we let the most primitive part of our brain respond to the cause of our fear, it leads to an automatic, overpowering urge to fight or run. If fear rules our decisions we are less productive at work. Worry occurs when we create mental unease by persistently engaging in disturbing thoughts. Worry can become self-escalating and self-perpetuating.

Example:

Bob was always worrying about what his employees thought of him. He would second-guess every decision he made and continually check with them about even the smallest issue, like what color he should paint his office. His employees did not respect him.

Avoiding Pain

We often want to avoid the pain that comes from facing problems. This makes us avoid facing challenges at work. Paradoxically, the problems get worse and so we try to avoid them more. This leads to a diminished sense of self-efficacy and self-respect that perpetuates failures and unhappiness.

Example:

Barbara continually felt harassed by a co-worker. The person put her down in meetings and went out of her way to point out Barbara's mistakes. Barbara didn't want to face the pain of a confrontation or possible retribution by complaining to her superior. Emboldened, the co-worker continued to heap on the abuse until Barbara quit her job.

Negative Self-image

Many people think poorly of themselves and their effectiveness at work. People who are very self-critical are often afraid to stop being so because they think they'll lose motivation. In fact, self-criticism leads to discouragement, dissatisfaction, and poor decision-making.

Example:

There was a woman who wrote a brilliant book on a particular topic and the CEO of a company asked her to work for him based on the strength of the book. She turned him down, thinking that she really didn't know that much; "after all," she reasoned, "anyone could write a book."

Unrealistic Expectations

Expectation is the condition of looking forward to a particular outcome. When we become overly caught up in an expectation we can get locked into a particular view of the future that limits our choices. Unrealistic expectation can lead to disappointment and discouragement. Unrealistic expectations destroy flexibility. It's OK to have an intention, a plan of action, but we can be limited when we have expectations that things should go a particular way. When we operate with detached intention we can let go of the image of how things are *supposed* to be.

Example:

Dave went away for a two-week vacation. He left with the expectation that his team would complete a complicated work assignment exactly as he would do it. When he returned, he found out that the job was successfully complete but they had achieved it in a radically different manner than he would have. When he expressed his disappointment to his employees for not following the proper procedure they reacted with hurt and frustration.

Blaming Others

When we blame others for mistakes or problems, we avoid looking at ourselves and taking responsibility. When people feel attacked, they tend to counterattack or shut down and hold resentment. It is always useful to consider the possibility that we are wrong.

Example:

An executive was very upset with one of his salespersons for missing an appointment and so he left the person a terse message about it. The supposedly errant person called back and sweetly said, "I had us down for the next day." When the executive checked, he saw that he had mistaken the date of the meeting.

When we do not use our emotional intelligence, we end up acting in ineffective and harmful ways. The more we allow our theorizing about life to be consciously informed by our emotions, the more we can overcome our blocks and the more effective and successful we will be. The goal is to let our emotions *inform* us rather than *deform* us. So, we need to bring our emotions more consciously into our decision-making.

Chapter 4

Assessing Your Emotionally Intelligent Leadership Skills

Here is a series of questions to help you assess the extent to which you lead in an emotionally intelligent way. Distribute copies of the blank questionnaire on the following pages to three to five people, asking each of them to answer these questions about you. Also, complete the questionnaire yourself.

Ask your colleagues to be completely honest about their answers. When you are answering these questions, try to be as honest with yourself as possible. Answer the questions as they apply to you **when you are at work.**

Please circle *one* number for each question.

Person being
assessed_____

1. It is easy for me to recognize what emotions I am experiencing in a particular situation.

very rarely	rarely			often	very often
1	2	3	4	5	6

2. At work, I appreciate other peoples' feelings and emotions.

very rarely	rarely			often	very often
1	2	3	4	5	6

3. I visualize a picture of what I want to create in the future.

very rarely	rarely			often	very often
1	2	3	4	5	6

4. When I commit to a plan, I carry it out.

very rarely	rarely			often	very often
1	2	3	4	5	6

5. I can be impulsive.

very rarely	rarely			often	very often
6	5	4	3	2	1

6. I spend time thinking about the broad perspective of a work situation.

very rarely	rarely			often	very often
1	2	3	4	5	6

7. I decide what I'm going to do based on my vision for the future.

very rarely	rarely			often	very often
1	2	3	4	5	6

8. When problems develop, I'll be there to help sort them out.

very rarely	rarely			often	very often
1	2	3	4	5	6

9. I develop clear intentions before I act.

very rarely	rarely			often	very often
1	2	3	4	5	6

10. It's difficult for me to consider my options when I get frustrated or angry.

very rarely	rarely			often	very often
6	5	4	3	2	1

11. I tend to get very involved and it makes it hard for me to be objective.

very rarely	rarely			often	very often
6	5	4	3	2	1

12. I examine the feelings, thoughts, and actions of others.

very rarely	rarely			often	very often
1	2	3	4	5	6

13. I ask myself, "What's the right thing to do here?"

very rarely	rarely			often	very often
1	2	3	4	5	6

14. People tell me I'm hard to talk to.

very rarely	rarely			often	very often
6	5	4	3	2	1

15. I go beyond standard procedures to solve a problem.

very rarely	rarely			often	very often
1	2	3	4	5	6

16. I resist changing my point of view.

very rarely	rarely			often	very often
6	5	4	3	2	1

17. I am open to all the possibilities in any given thought, act, or situation.

very rarely	rarely			often	very often
1	2	3	4	5	6

18. When I am fearful at work, I push through to achieve my goal.

very rarely	rarely			often	very often
1	2	3	4	5	6

19. At work it's hard to act independently and with accountability.

very rarely	rarely			often	very often
6	5	4	3	2	1

20. I communicate my vision for the future to those with whom I work.

very rarely	rarely			often	very often
1	2	3	4	5	6

21. I am able to speak my mind without getting others upset.

very rarely	rarely			often	very often
1	2	3	4	5	6

22. I recognize the choices inherent in a situation.

very rarely	rarely			often	very often
1	2	3	4	5	6

23. I take appropriate risks.

very rarely	rarely			often	very often
1	2	3	4	5	6

24. I am able to figure out the reasons behind different emotions.

very rarely	rarely			often	very often
1	2	3	4	5	6

25. It's hard to understand why others feel the way they do.

very rarely	rarely			often	very often
6	5	4	3	2	1

26. I can stay committed to a plan of action over a long period of time.

very rarely	rarely			often	very often
1	2	3	4	5	6

27. I am able to be flexible in dealing with others.

very rarely	rarely			often	very often
1	2	3	4	5	6

28. When I feel angry I can still stay composed.

very rarely	rarely			often	very often
1	2	3	4	5	6

29. When I speak or act I do so positively.

very rarely	rarely			often	very often
1	2	3	4	5	6

30. It's hard for me to realize when I am having different emotions.

very rarely	rarely			often	very often
6	5	4	3	2	1

31. I have a good understanding of why people act as they do.

very rarely	rarely			often	very often
1	2	3	4	5	6

32. If several people suggest a course of action that I don't necessarily agree with, I tend to keep my doubts to myself.

very rarely	rarely			often	very often
6	5	4	3	2	1

33. I focus on how I want things to be in the future.

very rarely	rarely			often	very often
1	2	3	4	5	6

34. In assessing a situation, I look at my biases and adjust my assessment accordingly.

very rarely	rarely			often	very often
1	2	3	4	5	6

35. If a needed action is not in my job description, I won't do it.

very rarely	rarely			often	very often
6	5	4	3	2	1

36. I'm very determined in completing what I set out to do.

very rarely	rarely			often	very often
1	2	3	4	5	6

37. When I think I'm right, I have a hard time listening to other people's alternative solutions.

very rarely	rarely			often	very often
6	5	4	3	2	1

38. I get inappropriately hung up on my emotional reaction.

very rarely	rarely			often	very often
6	5	4	3	2	1

39. I avoid whatever makes me afraid.

very rarely	rarely			often	very often
6	5	4	3	2	1

40. I act firmly, according to my core values.

very rarely	rarely			often	very often
1	2	3	4	5	6

41. I think about the long-term future when deciding what to do right now.

very rarely	rarely			often	very often
1	2	3	4	5	6

42. I watch how others react to me to better understand my own behavior.

very rarely	rarely			often	very often
1	2	3	4	5	6

43. When I try to solve a problem, I solicit choices and ideas from others.

very rarely	rarely			often	very often
1	2	3	4	5	6

44. In sizing up a situation, I get caught up in how I'd like things to be.

very rarely	rarely			often	very often
6	5	4	3	2	1

45. I think about the emotions behind my actions.

very rarely	rarely			often	very often
1	2	3	4	5	6

46. If I'm part of a group working on a task, I take responsibility for the group succeeding.

very rarely	rarely			often	very often
1	2	3	4	5	6

47. I say what I'm feeling no matter how it will impact others.

very rarely	rarely			often	very often
6	5	4	3	2	1

48. When I feel a strong impulse to do something, I generally pause to reflect and consider if I really want to act on it.

very rarely	rarely			often	very often
1	2	3	4	5	6

49. I take my "emotional temperature" before I make important decisions.

very rarely	rarely			often	very often
1	2	3	4	5	6

50. I try for a "win-win" solution whenever I speak or act.

very rarely	rarely			often	very often
1	2	3	4	5	6

To score the self-assessment, refer to the instructions in the Appendix on page 80. For action planning based on your scores, also see the Appendix on page 82.

Chapter 5

The Core
Skills

There are five core skills of emotional intelligence crucial to the success of any workplace endeavor, including effective leadership. These are:

➲ Knowing Yourself

➲ Maintaining Control

➲ Reading Others

➲ Perceiving Accurately

➲ Communicating with Flexibility

These five skills are not static. They interact constantly to help us make sound decisions as we respond to the ongoing demands of the workplace.

1. KNOWING YOURSELF

What is it?

- ➲ Recognizing your emotions

- ➲ Differentiating between emotions

- ➲ Knowing the reason behind the emotion

Knowing yourself means being in touch with your emotions, being able to recognize and understand them, and knowing what causes those emotions. When we experience a particular emotion in a situation, the emotion is a message, and we can deliberately respond to that message. In other words, we can use the information we are receiving from our reactions to situations.

Why is it useful?

Knowing your feelings and why you are having them allows you to evaluate a situation and make clearer decisions. It also helps you to understand your personal blocks to effective leadership. Take the case of Betty...

Betty was a middle manager at an insurance company who often seemed to shoot herself in the foot. Whenever the insurance claims in her group became backlogged, she felt fearful and automatically blamed her subordinates for the problem. Finally, her supervisor put her on probation for her poor management skills. Betty began to reflect on what she was doing or not doing which contributed to the continuing problems. She saw how her automatic blaming response prevented her from actively improving the procedures for processing claims.

Exercise:

Identify a recurrent leadership challenge at work that creates some sort of emotional tension for you.

_____

_____

_____

Picturing the challenging situation, write down the feelings and emotions that it brings up.

_____

_____

Now ask yourself, "Why am I having these feelings?" Keep asking the "why" behind the emotions.

_____

_____

_____

Based on your self-inquiry, write out some new ways to think and act in this situation.

_____

_____

2. MAINTAINING CONTROL

What is it?

- ➲ Resisting or delaying an impulse, drive, or temptation to act

- ➲ Controlling aggression, hostility, and irresponsible behavior

- ➲ Managing emotions in a flexible and adaptable way

Maintaining control is about staying calm amidst the chaos. When we maintain control we can stay composed even when there is a tight deadline and everyone else is snappish. The impact of losing control of our emotions can be far-reaching.

Fred was a senior manager who couldn't control his anger. Everyone avoided him and no one wanted to give him any bad news. Information was lost or learned too late, and poor performance built up.

Why is it useful?

Being able to maintain control can be crucial to the impact you have on others. If you communicate to employees that a work project is out of control, they will feel the same way. If you are able to present a sense of calm even in the face of crisis, those who follow you will gain new strength.

Exercise:

Right now, take a deep breath...Take another one. How does it feel?

We can consciously choose to perform simple actions which will change our emotional state.

The next time you become upset at work, pause and observe the thoughts you are having. If the thoughts are negative, rephrase them in the positive. Think about the type of supportive statements you would make to someone you care about. Use them with yourself.

Now picture the positive outcome you would like to achieve. Stay focused on that goal rather than the cause of your frustrations.

3. READING OTHERS

What is it?

➲ Being aware of the emotions of others

➲ Appreciating the emotions of others

➲ Understanding how and why people feel and act as they do

This skill is about relating to others' experiences. When we read others, we can engage them better in our vision. We can focus on the ways they can contribute to our vision. As we develop an appreciation for the emotions of others, we begin to reflect on our own feelings and behaviors as viewed through the eyes of others. We thus get a clearer perception of ourselves by how others react to us.

Why is it useful?

If you want to lead others effectively, being able to read their emotions and understand them can magnify your impact.

The Chief Operating Officer of a mid-sized hospital was a great visionary leader with an abundance of ideas and the energy to achieve them. The people who worked for him had great respect for his abilitites. However, because he never paid attention to the reactions of others, he would often get locked into ongoing, draining fights that limited his effectiveness.

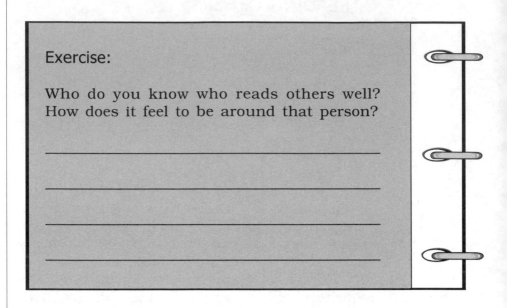

Exercise:

Who do you know who reads others well?
How does it feel to be around that person?

_____

_____

_____

_____

As with all the core skills, reading others takes practice. A particularly good time to practice reading others is when you are receiving feedback. So the next time you are receiving feedback from a colleague or someone to whom you report, try the following steps:

- ➲ Listen very carefully and as non-defensively as possible.

- ➲ Focus on what the other person may be feeling and thinking and why they are saying it.

- ➲ Restate what you think you heard and work with the other person until you have a clear grasp of his or her point of view.

4. PERCEIVING ACCURATELY

What is it?

- ➲ Accurately assessing a situation

- ➲ Having clear vision

- ➲ Keeping a broad perspective and being objective

Perceiving accurately is tapping into the emotional information available to us in a detached way so that we are able to assess a situation objectively. If we ignore our emotions, we discard key information, and those "blocked" emotions can distort our assessment of what is actually occurring. On the other hand, if we become too deeply caught up in our emotions, our perceptions will be distorted. Perceiving accurately requires us to scrutinize our biases and the filters through which we see our world.

Why is it useful?

When we are perceiving accurately we are able to make effective decisions about how to act. We are better able to consider our options and to make the right choices.

A man was riding on a train to work when he was approached by a young man who asked him the time. The older man said, "Drop dead!" After a moment of startled confusion the young man asked, "How could you be so rude to a stranger asking a perfectly innocent question?"

The older man said,

"I'm sorry. Have a seat and let me explain. If I were to tell you the time, we'd get into a conversation. We'd probably get along very well and I'd invite you home to my house for lunch. There you'd meet my wife and daughter. Now, you're obviously a very pleasant young man and my daughter is a lovely young woman, so you'd hit it off. The next thing I'd know, you'd be asking me for her hand in marriage. And I want you to know right now that I have no intention of letting my daughter marry a man who can't even afford a watch!"

Exercise:

If you are a second-level manager or higher, have meetings with workers at the bottom without their supervisors. These are called "skip-level" meetings. Before you meet with them, write out your view of their work situation. When you're meeting with them, take notes. Compare your initial thoughts with what you learned from them. Identify any assumptions or biases which may have kept you from perceiving accurately. Repeat this regularly.

If you are a first-level supervisor or below, have similar meetings with your suppliers, customers, or colleagues on a regular basis. Before you meet, write out what you think the situation is, take notes during the meeting, and compare to discover your biases.

5. COMMUNICATING WITH FLEXIBILITY

What is it?

- ➲ Having a full range of emotional expression

- ➲ Being authentic

- ➲ Addressing your needs as well as the needs of others

Through our understanding of our own emotions and those of others, we can be guided in how we communicate. If we stand up and say, "I'm really excited about this new initiative," but sound like we're really not, our audience will be guided by our nonverbal communication, not our words. We must be believed to be understood.

Why is it useful?

Effective leadership means getting others to do things because they *want* to do them. We can achieve this by being flexible in what we say and how we say it. It also means saying things in a way that respects that other person. An important component of communicating with flexibility is using non-verbal communication (body language) in a way that is truly aligned with our message.

43

As Suzette Elgin says in <u>Success with the Gentle Art of Verbal Self-Defense</u>, "Any words, be they ever so flawless, can have their meaning cancelled by body language--but not vice versa. There are no words capable of canceling the meaning transmitted by body language."[6] Being aware of our own body language and that of others gives us useful information to guide us in effective leadership.

Bob Stevens leaned forward with a small smile on his face and said very quietly, "I suppose I should be concerned about the way this project is heading." Harry Sands paid close attention to what his boss was saying. Was Bob really upset or was he just trying to make some sort of point with his words? He asked, "What exactly might concern you?"

Bob answered with a grimace, "The customer called me and said that he was generally pleased with the direction in which the work was going, but you didn't incorporate a suggestion he had about speeding up the schedule and he didn't understand why. I promised him I'd have a talk with you."

While nodding his head, Bob continued, "Harry, I feel happy with your work and I support you setting limits. The only thing I ask is that when the customer makes any kind of request you give him a very clear set of reasons for not honoring it. For instance, you might have told him the specifics for why you set up your time table as you did. Keep up the good work and let me know how your next conversation goes with the customer." Harry left feeling both supported and having a clearer idea of how to handle customers.

Exercise:

Think of the most important message you will communicate as a leader in the next week. For example you may have to introduce a new incentive plan or change a group's work assignment. Ask yourself, "What are the ramifications of what I am speaking about for me?"

_____

_____

What are the ramifications for those involved?

_____

_____

What are the emotions I want to communicate in that message?

_____

How do I want to communicate them?

_____

_____

Chapter 6

Developing the Core Skills

To aid in the process of strengthening our emotional intelligence we can actively use the EI Action Techniques. These are clear and simple tools for activating our emotional intelligence and strengthening the five core skills. We can apply them when we face any challenge at work.

The EI Action Techniques

➲ The PaRC Formula
➲ Core Connecting
➲ Syncing-In
➲ Focused Listening
➲ Re-Framing
➲ Process Communication

THE PaRC FORMULA

The PaRC formula is a clear-cut way to remember how to apply the skills of emotional intelligence. We can learn to "park" and put into neutral our automatic reactions to situations and make a more deliberate, contemplative response.

1. *Pause* **before reacting**
   Suspend action temporarily.
   Allow yourself to be deliberate.

2. *Reflect* **on the "what" and "why" of the feelings**
   Identify the emotion in yourself or others.
   Understand the "why" behind the emotion.

3. *Choose* **the appropriate thought or action**
   Act with the knowledge of your reflection.
   Think or act in a way that makes the situation work.

More about Pausing, Reflecting and Choosing

We can all learn the power of *pausing* or delay, the power to not react. If we simply refuse to react immediately, if we choose to reflect before we act, we buy the time to be deliberate in how we want to respond. In other words, we have a choice to not respond immediately. We don't have to be on automatic pilot.

To have that choice we must first be aware that something is occurring in and around us that needs attention. The first step is to use the power of awareness, of knowing that we're having a particular difficulty or impulse or feeling. Then we can begin to practice reflection.

There are two parts to *reflection*: identifying the emotion and understanding the why behind the emotion. It's about learning to know ourselves, our feelings and our reactions and working to read others' feelings and reactions. First we focus on identifying what we are feeling. Often more than one feeling is involved. Then, by continually asking ourselves: "Why might I be having these feelings?", or "Why might this person be reacting this way?", we delve deeper into the emotional message.

We are now in position to *choose* how we want to respond without resorting to old, unhelpful, patterns. By being fully aware of our internal responses, we can create new ways to view the situation and, possibly, develop new approaches that will contribute to success. The power to choose how we are going to think or act is an incredible freedom.

Doris, a senior manager of a sales team was told that a major sale had fallen through because of an employee's mishandling the negotiation. She was about to blast the employee in her usual way when she suddenly realized she had a choice... she could rant and rave over what happened, making herself and the employee miserable for the rest of the day. Or, she could see what could be learned from the mistake and shared with the whole team, and think about how to coach the employee one- on-one to improve his performance. That's what she chose to do.

The more we pause, reflect and consciously choose our thoughts and actions the more effective we become, and the more our performance can improve.

CORE CONNECTING

Core connecting is a way to regain our composure, focus, and energy when we are side-tracked or distracted. It's about letting go of whatever we are caught up in and bringing our focus inside for a moment to help reorient and reconnect with our inner foundation. The breath can serve as a powerful tool to help us with our shift in focus.

1. **Take *3 slow, deep breaths***
   As you breathe, focus on the air as it flows in and out.

2. **Become aware of *the next thought that pops up in your head***
   It doesn't matter what the thought is.

3. **Say to yourself, "*I am having a thought about......*(restate the thought)"**

4. **Take *3 more slow, deep breaths***

SYNCING-IN

Syncing-in is a technique that improves performance by heightening our awareness of a situation and helping us to respond at an intuitive level. It's about tapping into information we already have. Our intuition gives us knowledge without step-by-step cognitive reasoning. Antonio Damasio, a renowned neurologist, calls intuition,

> *"...a mysterious mechanism by which we arrive at the solution of a problem without reasoning toward it."*

1. **Have a *beginner's mind***
   Clear your mind of preconceptions and prejudgments.

2. **Focus fully on your *immediate experience***
   Stay alert, tune into your body, attend to your senses, be completely present.

3. ***Continually re-engage* in what you are doing**
   Keep bringing your attention back to what's at hand.

FOCUSED LISTENING

Focused listening means paying concentrated attention to what someone else is saying. We first need to be willing to pay attention to what is motivating or influencing the other person. To do this we need to let go of our personal agenda and choose to focus on theirs.

It is important to recognize that listening is different from agreeing. Also, we speak more slowly than we think, so we can use this extra thinking time to go deeper into the other person's message.

1. **_Expand_ your reception**
   Be open to picking up all possible information. Be aware of the subtle shades of meaning being expressed.

2. **_Step_ into the other person's shoes**
   Imagine yourself in the other person's place. Think about how they must feel about what they are describing.

3. **_Dig_ deeper into the message**
   Use your extra thinking time to hypothesize about the core message of what's being communicated. Anticipate where they might be going next.

RE-FRAMING

Re-framing is shifting our focus from a limiting image of how the world works to a more inclusive one. It's attaching new meaning to a situation, presenting a new context for issues. It is not sugar coating. It's creating a new interpretation of a situation that can lead us to solutions.

Albert Einstein said,

"Problems cannot be solved by thinking within the framework in which the problems were created."

The steps of re-framing involve asking different types of questions to come up with a new meaning to a situation.

1. *Identify* **your current frame**
   Out loud or in writing, make a succinct statement describing your current framework of the situation. Ask yourself, "How does this frame limit me? Where does this frame lead me?"

2. *Look* **into the future**
   What might a desired future look, sound and feel like? What would this situation/task/experience look like if it were to end successfully?

3. *Explore* **new frames**
   How might this situation be an opportunity? What's the flip side to the negative aspects of this situation/task/experience? How would an unbiased observer describe this situation?

53

PROCESS COMMUNICATION

The "process" is the underlying movement behind an interaction. The content is the topic of an interaction. Process is usually implicit. When we practice process communication, we shine a light on what's usually important but may be unspoken. Process comments can be made about overall situations, underlying patterns, feelings, relationships, or agendas.

1. **Pay attention to *body language***
   This includes the tone or volume of the voice, facial gestures, posture, and hand gestures. Much of our emotional communication is nonverbal.

2. ***Identify what is happening,* not what is being discussed**
   This usually involves the emotions around an interaction.

3. **Make a clear, non-attacking *process comment***
   Be specific and descriptive.

Chapter 7

The Higher-Order Skills

The core skills of emotional intelligence are necessary but not sufficient for effective leadership. Let's look at the additional skills needed. All of the higher-order skills are about making an emotional connection with others. To make that emotional connection and to lead them, we need to inspire others by:

➲ Taking Responsibility

➲ Generating Choices

➲ Embracing a Vision

➲ Having Courage

➲ Demonstrating Resolve

Practicing the higher-order skills requires effort and a willingness to leave our comfort zone. By practicing them, we inspire others.

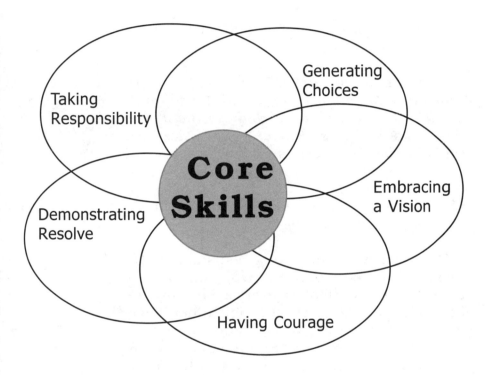

1. TAKING RESPONSIBILITY

What is it?

- ⮑ Taking responsibility is acting independently and with accountability

- ⮑ It's about ownership of a problem as well as a solution

Andy Pearson, past CEO of PepsiCo and founding chairman of Tricon Global Restaurant, Inc., the largest restaurant chain in the world, doesn't just sit in his office and give orders. He regularly visits his company's restaurants and seeks contact and input from employees from all levels. He operates from an internal frame of reference that promotes taking responsibility in the broadest posible way.

The framework for taking responsibility is based on our core values. Our core values serve as the point of reference for how we act and work. Margaret Wheatley in her book, Leadership and the New Science writes of the pervasive organizing power of self-reference.[8] When a situation calls for a response we can base it upon our system of inner values to maintain a sense of our own integrity and self-renewal.

Why is it useful?

It's hard to follow someone you don't respect. When we see a person who takes responsibility for his or her actions and doesn't shirk from a challenge just because the situation is not specified in his or her job description, we appreciate that person.

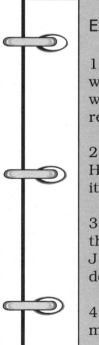

Exercise:

1. Start a list of all the agreements you have made with others at work. For example, "I told Bob that I would look for opportunities to give him more responsibilities."

2. Evaluate the current status of that agreement. Has it been fullfilled? Are you actively working at it? Has it fallen by the wayside?

3. Make an action point for each agreement. With the previous example, it might be, "Talk to Harry Jones about giving part of the work process development program to Bob."

4. Keep an ongoing log of your agreements as you make them. Periodically review them.

2. GENERATING CHOICES

What is it?

- ⮑ Generating choices means opening ourselves to the varied possibilities in any given thought, act, or situation.

- ⮑ Emotionally intelligent leadership depends on being able to discover the available choices in any given situation and to help others recognize those choices.

Why is it useful?

When we offer choices to others we build commitment and ownership in our ideas. We also become open to new possibilities upon which to build.

Bill Marriott writes about how his father created a whole new direction for his firm's business.

> "In 1937, while visiting the Hot Shoppe adjacent to the old Hoover airfield on the outskirts of Washington, he noticed customers buying sandwiches.... Travelers wanted to eat on the plane...the world's largest airline catering business was born. All because my father was on the scene and had his eyes open to new opportunities." [9]

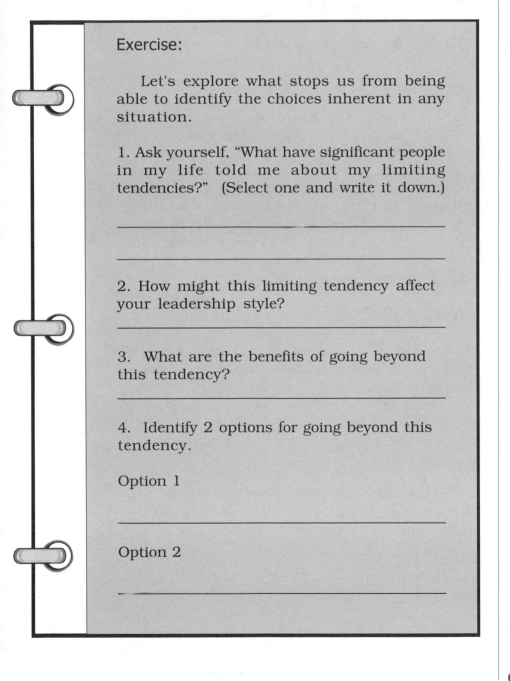

Exercise:

Let's explore what stops us from being able to identify the choices inherent in any situation.

1. Ask yourself, "What have significant people in my life told me about my limiting tendencies?" (Select one and write it down.)

_____

_____

2. How might this limiting tendency affect your leadership style?

_____

3. What are the benefits of going beyond this tendency?

_____

4. Identify 2 options for going beyond this tendency.

Option 1

_____

Option 2

_____

3. EMBRACING A VISION

What is it?

⮞ Embracing a vision is fully committing ourselves to a particular view of the future.

⮞ To be fully embraced, a vision needs to permeate communications and guide actions.

When we embrace a vision we give others something to aspire to. It's hard to embrace a vision. It might feel constraining and limiting. But in fact a vision creates clarity and direction that builds energy and provides a clear path for all to commit to.

Why is it useful?

Howard Schultz, Chairman and CEO of Starbucks Coffee Company had the vision to create a sense of community in all his stores, so that Starbucks would become the third place in America between home and work. He embraced this vision fully and shared it with the people who worked at his company.

A vision doesn't have to be created by you. But you do want to select one that is compelling and credible.

Exercise:

1. Select a vision for your particular workgroup. Think about what the desired future would look like. Remember that it should be a vision that you can willingly and actively embrace.

_____

_____

_____

2. Identify what current factors would support that vision.

_____

_____

_____

3. Identify what current factors would block the vision.

_____

_____

_____

4. Given your findings, what are some initiatives that you can start which will communicate the vision and bring it to fruition.

_____

_____

_____

4. HAVING COURAGE

What is it?

Courage is not the absence of fear but rather the judgement that something else is more important than fear. When we approach our work with fear we cannot lead. As author and consultant Robert Terry says, "fear extinguishes leadership."[10]

As an emotionally intelligent leader we need to have the courage to:

- ➲ look at our choices and ourselves

- ➲ take responsibility

- ➲ buck trends and standard modes of operation

- ➲ make tough decisions

Why is it useful?

Emotionally intelligent leadership means having the courage to find the best possible outcome to every situation. It may mean challenging the status quo or going against what is popular. It takes courage to say, "I don't know" and to be willing to learn from your failures.

Beth, Vice President of Marketing at an international processed food company, was afraid of her new CEO. Everything would be going along fine and then he'd suddenly belittle something she said, often in front of other people.

During a strategic planning meeting with all the senior executives, it happened again. Beth had been describing a new idea for organizing her team. The CEO said, "That's not a very sensible idea." Everyone grew silent and the energy from a good morning's session drained away.

Beth felt deflated, but she told herself that it was a good idea and she shouldn't just let the idea go. She reminded herself that the CEO had often changed his mind about other projects. She also realized that if she were able to implement the new plan, it would make her life a lot easier. So, she brought it up again. She said, "I know on the surface it might seem difficult to put into place, but the savings to our company could be enormous." He reviewed the many benefits and asked that the idea be revisited at the next executive staff meeting.

Exercise:

Think of a time when you felt really stuck and fearful at work and were eventually able to push through it. Ask yourself how you generated the courage to move forward.

Describe what happened:

_____

_____

_____

What gave you the courage to move forward?

_____

_____

_____

_____

Exercise:

Select a situation where you wish to lead at work but have not yet taken the step. Perhaps one of your fears or limiting tendencies has stopped you. It might have to do with influencing a team in a certain direction or trying out a new idea. Briefly write out a description of the situation.

_____

_____

_____

Write out what would help you to call forth your courage to take that step.

_____

_____

_____

_____

5. DEMONSTRATING RESOLVE

What is it?

- ⮑ Regularly making decisions about what to do, with firm determination

- ⮑ Demonstrating to others your commitment to a plan of action

Demonstrating resolve involves making a sustained self-effort. When we act with firm resolution we build our inner strength and direction. Without resolve we can feel helpless, alienated from our work, cynical, worthless, and weak.

Why it is useful?

When resolved, we create a sense of control and self-determination. It builds self-confidence, self-esteem and a sense of personal effectiveness that enhances the possibility for success.

Demonstrating resolve entails operating with clear intentions. When we show firmness of purpose we inspire others. Demonstrating resolve communicates the meaning and significance of the organization's work. It creates motivation in others.

Leaders are generally inundated by continuous demands and crises. Resolve helps us to maintain our focus and keep on track. We can't make a difference overnight. Real organizational change takes years. Change takes resolve.

Exercise:

Identify one aspect of your work that you would like to stay focused on for at least three months. For example:
- Developing a more efficient system of accountability within your work group.
- Implementing an initiative to increase team-based operations within your organization

Now, in your planner, make a series of notations at the beginning of each week for the next three months about the aspect of your work that you decided to focus on. This will remind you to spend some time on this aspect of your work. On a date three months away, write this question, "How's it going with the work I resolved to focus on three months ago?"

Chapter 8

Developing the Higher-Order Skills

The Leadership Action Techniques have been developed to help us improve the higher-order skills.

The Leadership Action Techniques

- ➲ Responsibility Checklist
- ➲ Choice Building
- ➲ Vision Linking
- ➲ Lighting the Fire
- ➲ Firming Up

Practiced on a regular basis, these techniques will help to bolster our emotionally intelligent leadership.

RESPONSIBILITY CHECKLIST

To build a framework for taking responsibility, we can ask ourselves questions about our actions. Taking responsibility includes investing our energy in leading those who work with us.

1. **Am I making a *contribution*?**

2. **Am I fully *accepting the consequences* of the actions I've taken?**

3. **In light of my subordinates' reactions, is what I am doing discouraging them or *uplifting them*?**

4. **Based on my actions thus far, *whom am I serving*?**

These are not easy questions. It takes time to even ask them. However, by doing the asking, we orient ourselves towards taking responsibility in a work activity.

"A new moral principle is emerging which holds that the only authority deserving one's allegiances is that which is freely granted by the led to the leader in response to and in proportion to the clearly evident servant stature of the leader."[11]

Robert Greenleaf

CHOICE BUILDING

When under demand, our tendency is to reach a quick resolution to a problem. Often, this leads to considering only a small range of choices. Here are some steps to generate choices.

1. *Let go*
   Let go of the need to be recognized as always being right.
   Let go of having the only valid solution.
   Let go of the need to control.

2. **Actively *solicit choices* from others**
   Try not to criticize failure or unfamiliar ideas.

3. ***Invite ideas from outside* your current experiences and culture**
   Examine ideas even though they seem silly or incongruous at face value.

"Decision makers should also encourage trusted advisors to confront them when the advisors see them behaving defensively."[12]

Chris Argyris

VISION LINKING

A vision can weave throughout our daily life and become a part of us. To achieve this, we need to keep remembering the vision. This maintains focus on our goal and creates a foundation for all our efforts.

1. **Select a vision that you can *willingly and actively embrace***

2. ***Use metaphors* to make your vision more accessible to others**
   Create vivid images that represent your vision.

3. ***Own it and live it***
   Show that you care about reaching that vision.

4. ***Incorporate the vision* into your daily speech**

"...developing a vision is an exercise of both the head and the heart..."[13]

John Kotter

LIGHTING THE FIRE

When you light a fire in a fireplace, it helps to ignite the paper and kindling under the wood in several different places to make the fire grow and be sustained. We can light the fire of our courage by igniting it at several points.

1. *Recognize* **what you are afraid of**
   Are you afraid of rejection, failure, embarrassment, or loss of control?

2. *Focus on the benefits* **of taking the risk**
   Don't focus on the fear.

3. *Tolerate* **the discomfort**
   Go beyond your comfort zone.

4. *Practice* **by envisioning the steps to success**

"Leading from a clear, personal sense of purpose creates courage; real courage attracts real followers."[14]

Richard Leider

FIRMING UP

Demonstrating resolve involves sustaining effort through continual recommitment. We can keep finding new ways to get things done.

1. **Choose *reachable and worthwhile long-term goals***
   These should be in line with your core values.

2. **Build in *short-term targets***
   This allows for a series of successes as you move toward your long-term goal.

3. **Develop a *support network* for your intention**
   Find people who can get behind the vision so that the vision grows.

4. ***Anticipate and prepare* for difficulties and obstacles**
   Plan for the unexpected.

5. **Continually *renew your resolutions***

"Exceptional people have made continual sacrifices... because they chose an angle and stuck reasonably to it. Ultimately, it is this relentless dedication that engages trust."[15]

Warren Bennis & Burt Nanus

By applying the skills outlined in this handbook, you can improve how you lead and increase your success in your organization. How you apply these skills will vary based on who you are, your organization, specific job, and work environment.

If you bring emotionally intelligent leadership into your organization, colleagues will appreciate your contribution. Invite its development in others. Then you will help create a high-performing organization that is able to change and lead into the future.

Scoring the Assessment and Action Planning

Scoring the Assessment (on P. 23)

➲ Write down your score for the five items listed under each category. Total them. Thus, if you had scores of 4, 5, 4, 2 and 3 for the five "Knowing Yourself" questions [1, 24,30, 45, and 49], your total would be 18.

➲ Circle the corresponding digit or dot from 5 - 30 to show your total. (In the example, you'd circle 18.)

➲ Draw a line between the scores for the 10 categories to create a graph.

The Core Skills

Knowing Yourself 5 . . . .10 . . . .15 . . . .20 . . . .25 30
(1, 24, 30, 45, 49) ___ + ___ + ___ + ___ + ___ = ___

Maintaining   5 . . . .10 . . . .15 . . . .20 . . . .25 30
Control
(5, 10, 28, 38, 48) ___ + ___ + ___ + ___ + ___ = ___

Reading Others   5 . . . .10 . . . .15 . . . .20 . . . .25 30
(2, 12, 25, 31, 42) ___ + ___ + ___ + ___ + ___ = ___

Perceiving   5 . . . .10 . . . .15 . . . .20 . . . .25 30
Accurately
(6, 11, 16, 34, 44) ___ + ___ + ___ + ___ + ___ = ___

Communicating   5 . . . .10 . . . .15 . . . .20 . . . .25 30
with Flexibility
(14, 21, 29, 47, 50) ___ + ___ + ___ + ___ + ___ = ___

The Higher-Order Skills

Taking   5 . . . .10 . . . .15 . . . .20 . . . .25 30
Responsibility
(8, 13, 19, 35, 46) ___ + ___ + ___ + ___ + ___ = ___

Generating   5 . . . .10 . . . .15 . . . .20 . . . .25 30
Choices
(17, 22, 27, 37, 43) ___ + ___ + ___ + ___ + ___ = ___

Embracing a   5 . . . .10 . . . .15 . . . .20 . . . .25 30
Vision
(3, 7, 20, 33, 41)   ___ + ___ + ___ + ___ + ___ = ___

Having Courage   5 . . . .10 . . . .15 . . . .20 . . . .25 30
(15, 18, 23, 32, 39) ___ + ___ + ___ + ___ + ___ = ___

Demonstrating   5 . . . .10 . . . .15 . . . .20 . . . .25 30
Resolve
(4, 9, 26, 36, 40)   ___ + ___ + ___ + ___ + ___ = ___

Action Planning Based on Your Assessment Scores

Total the responses from your colleagues. Add the five item scores together for each category and divide by the number of colleagues. Plot the average responses of your colleagues as you did for your answers (tip: use a different colored pen for your colleagues responses.)

Identify any gaps between your scores and your colleagues' average score. Describe below.

_____

_____

_____

_____

Identify the areas you would most like to improve upon.

_____

_____

_____

_____

_____

_____

_____

Write out an action plan to improve upon these areas. (Use the tips in the handbook as a guide.)

_____

_____

_____

_____

_____

_____

_____

_____

_____

_____

_____

_____

_____

NOTES

1. James MacGregor Burns, *Leadership.* (p. 44). New York: Harper and Row, 1978.

2. P. B.Vail, *Managing as a Performing Art: New Ideas for a World of Chaotic Change.* (p. 2). San Francisco: Jossey-Bass, 1989.

3. R.Bar-On, *BarOn Emotional Quotient Inventory: A Measure of Emotional Intelligence. User's Manual.* Toronto: Multi-Health Systems, Inc., 1997.

4. See Washington Post, 10/26/97.

5. R.Bar-On, *BarOn Emotional Quotient Inventory.*

6. Suzette Elgin, *Success with the Gentle Art of Self-Defense.* NY: Prentice Hall, 1989.

7. Antonio R. Damasio, *Descartes' Error: Emotion, Reason, and the Human Brain. New York:* G. P. Putnam's Sons, 1994.

8. Margaret J. Wheatley, *Leadership and the New Science: Learning about Organization from an Orderly Universe.* San Francisco: Berrett-Koehler Publishers, 1992.

9. J.W. Marriott, Jr. and Kathi Ann Brown, *A Spirit to Serve: Marriott's Way.* New York, HarperCollins, 1997.

10. Robert W. Terry, *Authentic Leadership: Courage in Action.* (p. 237). San Francisco: Jossey-Bass, 1993.

11. Robert Greenleaf, *Servant Leadership: A Journey into the Nature of Legitimate Power and Greatness.* (p. 10). New York: Paulist Press, 1977.

12. Chris Argyris, *Knowledge for Action: A Guide to Overcoming Barriers to Organizational Change.* (p. 6). San Francisco, Jossey-Bass, 1993.

13. John Kotter, *Leading Change* (p. 79). Boston, Massachusetts, Harvard Business School Press, 1996

14. Richard Leider, "The Ultimate Leadership Task", in F. Hesselbein, M. Goldsmith, R. Beckhard, eds., *The Leader of the Future*, (p. 195). San Francisco, Jossey-Bass, 1996.

15. Warren Bennis & Burt Nanus, *Leaders: The strategies for Taking Charge.* p. 45. New York, Harper & Row, 1985.

SUGGESTED READING

Burns, James MacGregor. *Leadership.* New York: Harper and Row, 1978.

Damasio, Antonio R. *Descartes' Error: Emotion, Reason, and the Human Brain. New York:* G. P. Putnam's Sons, 1994.

Ekman, Paul and Davidson, Richard J. (Eds.) *The Nature of Emotion: Fundamental Questions.* New York: Oxford University Press, 1994.

Goleman, Daniel. *Emotional Intelligence: Why it can matter more than IQ.* New York: Bantam, 1995.

Greenleaf, R. *Servant Leadership: A Journey into the Nature of Legitimate Power and Greatness.* New York: Paulist Press, 1977.

Kotter, J. *Leading Change.* Boston: Harvard Business School Press, 1996.

Kouzes, James M. and Posner, Barry Z. *Credibility: How Leaders Gain and Lose it, Why People Demand It.* San Francisco: Jossey-Bass Publishers, 1993.

Kouzes, James M. and Posner, Barry Z. *The Leadership Challenge: How to Keep Getting Extraordinary Things Done in Organizations.* San Francisco: Jossey-Bass Publishers, 1995.

Sternberg, Robert J. *Successful Intelligence: How Practical and Creative Intelligence Determine Success in Life.* New York: Plume, 1997.

Terry, Robert W. *Authentic Leadership: Courage in Action.* San Francisco: Jossey-Bass, 1993.

Tichy, Noel M. *The Leadership Engine: How Winning Companies Build Leaders at Every Level.* New York: HarperCollins, 1997.

Vail, Peter B. *Managing as a Performing Art: New Ideas for a World of Chaotic Change.* San Francisco: Jossey-Bass, 1989.

Wheatley, Margaret J. *Leadership and the New Science: Learning about Organization from an Orderly Universe.* San Francisco: Berrett-Koehler Publishers, 1992.

Wren, J. Thomas (Ed.). *The Leadership Companion.* New York: The Free Press, 1995.

Order Form

The Handbook of Emotionally Intelligent Leadership

TO ORDER BY PHONE:
1.800.511.6150

TO ORDER BY FAX:
1.877.246.5908

E-MAIL: dafeldman@leadershipperformance.com

WEBSITE: www.leadershipperformance.com

Pricing		Shipping and Handling	
1-9 Books	$11.95 ea.	1-2 Book (First Class)	$4.50
10-99	$10.95 ea.	3-15 Books (UPS)	$8.00
100 +	$9.50 ea.	6-100 Books (UPS)	$16.00

Quantity	Subtotal	Shipping and Handling	Total
_____	_____	_____	_____

Shipping Information

Name..

Organization..

Address..

City...State..........Zip.........

Phone....................................Fax...

Check.....Visa.....MC.....AMEX......

Card #...
exp. date.........

Signature...

Cardholder...

Daniel Feldman, Ph.D., President of Leadership Performance Solutions, Inc. is a consulting psychologist who, for over twenty years, has served as a catalyst for change in organizations. Dr. Feldman coaches senior staff and facilitates meetings and retreats at large and small private sector companies and has led organization-wide transformation interventions at federal agencies. He is the author of *The Manager's Pocket Guide to Workplace Coaching* by HRD Press, and *Critical Thinking: Strategies for Decision Making* by Crisp Publications. Dr. Feldman is a frequent speaker on the topics of leadership, strategic thinking, and coaching.

Leadership Performance Solutions, Inc. offers a variety of consulting services including: leadership development, executive coaching, group facilitation, team development, strategic planning, conflict resolution, process improvement, change management and training programs.